# RADSPORTS GUIDES

# IN-LINE SKATING

## TRACY NELSON MAURER

Rourke Publishing LLC
Vero Beach, Florida 32964

www.rourkepublishing.com

Project Assistance:
Cathi Austin, Health Enhancement Coordinator at the Superior-Douglas County Family YMCA in Superior, WI, also teaches in-line skating clinics. A member of the Northern In-line Skaters Club, she participates in marathons and other in-line skating events.

The author also extends appreciation to Mike Maurer, Kendall and Lois M. Nelson, Harlan Maurer, Dana Wheelock, and Drs. Steven Massopust, Timothy Rich, and Boyd Erdman.

Photo Credits – Pages 4, 12, 33©Jaimie Squire/Allsport; pages 11, 30 ©Nathan Bilow/Allsport; page 17©Eyewire; page 37©Simon Bruty/Allsport; page 41©Jed Jacobsohn/Allsport; page 43; page 43©Jon Ferry/Allsport

Editorial Services:
Pamela Schroeder

**Library of Congress Cataloging-in-Publication Data**

Maurer, Tracy Nelson
        In-line Skating / Tracy Nelson Maurer
            p. cm. — (Radsports guides)
        Includes bibliographical references and index.
        Summary: Surveys the history, equipment, techniques, and safety factors of in-line skating.
        ISBN 1-58952-103-X
        1. In-line skating—Juvenile literature. [1. In-line skating.] I. Title.

GV859.73 .M392001
796.21—dc21                                              2001041656

Printed in the USA

# TABLE OF CONTENTS

*Hard-charging, aggressive skaters add excitement to the sport.*

# LAME NAME, COOL SPORT

In-line skating is a lame name for a cool sport. But don't call it Rollerblading either. Rollerblades are a brand of in-line skates, just like Kleenex is a brand of tissue. You don't go Kleenexing your nose do you?

The name sounds stuffy. Even so, in-line skating is one of America's fastest growing sports. Millions of people in-line skate for fun, for transportation, or to stay fit

chapter

## ONE

Some athletes use in-line skates to train for other sports like ice hockey or skiing. Advanced skaters may race. Hard-core skaters might work into **aggressive skating**, or aggro-skating. They do jumps, spins, and other flashy moves.

## A NEW SPORT ON A ROLL

Before the mid-1980s in-line skating, as you know it, did not exist. Some skates invented in the 1960s came close, but they were too hard to control. They never got popular.

In 1979 a pair of those early in-line skates caught the attention of two young brothers from Minnesota, Scott and Brennan Olson. They wanted to play hockey during the summer and saw a way to make the clunky old in-line skates work. The brothers used the boots from their hockey skates for more comfort and better control. Most importantly, they added a rubber heel brake to the design. Now people could stop—and the sport could start.

Five years later, a new company took over the brothers' design and Rollerblade made the sport famous. Now you see in-line skates all over the world. Many other companies make in-line skates today, too.

## DARLING TO DARING SKATES

The Olson brothers probably never dreamed that in-line skates with darling neon-pink swirls would sell. Today people buy skates in pink, purple, and blue—any color you can imagine. More than colors and patterns, in-line skates now come in a variety of styles to fit different uses, **terrains** and skills.

All of the big companies make specialty skates, too. Some skates have vents for people with hot feet. Others feature wheels that roll easily over rough roads. Off-road models even broke onto the scene.

## Kids' Skates
- 3 or 4 wheels
- Paved driveways and pathways or skate parks
- New or some skills

Smaller feet need smaller skates, not less quality. Watch out for wimpy plastic straps that break or tear off easily. The skates should have a brake pad. Look for 70mm wheels you can replace. Some kids' skates now come with adjustable boots to fit growing feet.

## Racing Skates
- 4 or 5 wheels
- Smoothly paved pathways or streets
- Advanced skills

These skates deliver speed, speed, and more speed. They look like they're flying when they're still in the box. Racers give up some turning control with the long wheelbase of these high-performance skates.

## Recreational Skates
- 3 or 4 wheels
- Paved pathways, streets, or skate parks
- New or some skills

Skaters cruising paved pathways or streets enjoy the comfort and control recreational skates provide. The shorter wheelbase makes turning easier. These skates work well for gliders, cross-trainers, and fitness buffs. They usually have a brake pad or some other braking system.

## Aggro- or Street Skates
- 4 wheels
- Streets, urban areas, skate parks
- Advanced skills

Street skates look very different on the bottom. Aggro-skaters go without a brake pad. They stop by dragging their wheels. Extra grind plates, bolted onto the bottoms, wear off instead of the skate base. A centered H-shaped block lets skaters grind, or slide, on metal rails, curbs, and other props. Some anti-rockered skates use two smaller middle wheels for grinds.

*Skate shops offer many skate styles. Choose skates
that fit well and match your skills.*

## TEST DRIVE YOUR WHEELS

You can join the sport without dropping major dollars. Some entry-level skates cost only $20 or so at discount stores.

The price climbs with quality, comfort, and specialty designs. Racing or street skates may cost well over $200 at skate shops. These stores usually offer more selections and sizes than stores selling entry-level skates.

Don't skimp on the fit. Skates should wrap snugly around your feet for good control (and fewer blisters). Your toes should loosely touch the front of the boot, but your heel shouldn't move. The skate shop staff can help you match the skates to your skills, skating area, and skating style.

## LACES OR BUCKLES?

Laces or buckles? Both? Buy the skates that fit best for you. Recreational skaters tend to like buckles because buckles adjust quickly. They also stay put. Buckles often cost more than laces.

Lower price makes laces sound good. Also, laces don't pinch or bind in one spot like buckles can do. Then again, laces loosen after awhile and you must stop to tighten them.

What if you pick laces and decide you don't like them later? Some stores sell buckles to replace, or **retrofit**, the laces.

**RAD TIP**

### Deals On Wheels
Many shops take trade-ins and sell them at low prices. Check the used bearings, wheels, and brakes very carefully. Watch for pre-season sales to save on new skates when the selection is better. End-of-season sales might have lower prices but fewer sizes available.

9

## GEAR UP FOR FALLING DOWN

Your skull wasn't built to handle crashes on cement curbs or asphalt streets. Those kinds of falls can cause lasting brain damage (or worse).

Both new and advanced in-line skaters should always wear brain buckets. New skaters tend to fall backwards or straight down, sometimes breaking bones. Advanced skaters fall less often, but their wipe outs hit hard and fast. A lot of skate parks, skate centers, and racecourses will not allow you to skate without a **helmet**. In New York and Oregon, children and teens must wear helmets by law.

Bike helmets work for bike riders. Buckle your brains into a multi-impact in-line skater's helmet. Look for an official sticker on the helmet that says the design meets safety standards. Also, make sure the helmet sits snugly on your head.

## HANDS DOWN PROTECTION

**Wrist guards** wrap around your hands and wrists. A flattened bar fits into the palm of each hand. This hard plastic bar slides across asphalt, so you leave less skin on the pavement. The guards also keep your wrists from snapping backward, twisting, or otherwise ruining your day.

Knee and elbow pads also use hard plastic shells to take the impact of a fall. Put them on tightly enough so that they won't slip off when you skid across the pavement.

Think about wearing digger-friendly pants and long sleeves, too. You don't have to look like your mama dressed you, but make sure nothing can catch in the wheels. Dress for the weather. Watch out for windbreakers or other waterproof clothes that trap sweat.

HELMET

WRIST GUARDS

ELBOW PADS

KNEE PADS

SKATES

*Knowing how to handle a fall can make it less painful.*
*Always stand up and wave to the gawkers afterwards.*

# CRASH COURSE ON CRASHING

In-line skaters experience about five types of falls, not one of which is fun. But you can make crashing less painful if you know what to do.

### 1. Face-plants

Face-plants are one way to stop quickly, but they often reshape your nose and teeth. Fortunately, new skaters usually fall backwards (see butt-plants below). Try to keep your hands over your face when you fall.

### 2. Prayers

At slower speeds you can fall safely on your knee pads, like you're saying prayers (which some new skaters also do). Bend your knees and drop onto your knee pads. Don't tense your wrists—let the wrist guards scrape the pavement for you.

### 3. Butt-plants

New skaters often plop on their bottoms. Try not to stop the fall with your hands—that's what cracks wrists. Falling backwards too hard can also break your tailbone. Instead, drop and roll, so the impact moves across your body.

### 4. Bacon Frying In A Pan

Fast skaters and aggro-skaters look like they're getting tossed around like bacon when they fall. They mean to do that. By rolling with the fall, they reduce the impact. In a fast fall, try to keep your body loose with your hands near your face or over your head. Fall uphill if you can.

### 5. Collisions

Some people try to brake by smacking into walls, buildings, signs, cars, or trees. This works, but it hurts. When you can't avoid a collision, try to relax your body. Keep your arms and legs loose. They act as shock absorbers for your joints.

## ROAD RASH

Some skaters glide along like pokey tourists. Usually, they tumble too slowly to do major damage. Someday you might skate with speed and you may even try tricks. Then expect to collect scabs.

No matter how much armor, or padding, you wear, scrapes happen to daring in-line skaters. Most road rash looks gross, but it's not serious. Wash it gently, put on **antiseptic** cream or spray, and let it scab over. The scab might feel tight and break when you skate. Try covering the scab with a thin layer of petroleum jelly to soften it before you go out.

Most road rash doesn't need gauze unless you think you might wipe out and fill it full of dirt again. If it's really gnarly looking, you can also put on a bandage for going out in public.

## DOCTOR IT UP

See a doctor if you can't wash the dirt, gravel, or glass out of the road rash. Or, if the scrape looks deep and meaty, don't mess around. Go to the doctor. Untreated wounds can become infected.

Also, a severe head-banging may make you see stars. Sit down and put your head between your knees. If your vision stays cloudy or if you feel stabbing pains anywhere, ask someone to bring you to the doctor right away.

**RAD TIP**

**First Aid First**
For long rides or a full day at the skate park, bring a water bottle and wear a fanny pack with first-aid supplies. Fill it with large bandages, gauze pads, antiseptic wipes, and antiseptic ointment.

# STOP BEFORE YOU GO

Put a pair of fancy, new tennis shoes on a toddler, and the little kid really believes the shoes make him run faster. Some people never grow up. They believe expensive in-line skates and gear are all they need to skate like a pro.

Pros started out as wobbly beginners. They learned to use their skates correctly and safely. What separates the pros from the crowd? Practice. Now you know the secret.

chapter
TWO

## BUNNIES IN THE GRASS

Bunnies, or frightened new skaters, cling to benches, trees and even other skaters. They often walk in grass where the skate wheels won't spin.

It's OK to use the grass at first to practice your **stance**. Stand with your feet about 6 inches (15.24 cm) apart. Keep your arms and hands in front where you can see them. Bend your knees so your shins press against the skate front. Steady your weight on the arches of your feet.

Try the "Bunny-Hop Stop" in the grass, too. Roll slowly from the pavement onto the grass. The wheels stop right away. Your body does not. It lunges forward at the same speed as before. The trick? As soon as you hit the grass, start hopping or run into the lawn. Keep your knees bent. Thank your padding.

Always clear the grass, mud, and other gunk out of your wheels before rolling onto the pavement.

## LESSONS MAKE SENSE

Take a lesson if you really want to know how to in-line skate. You'll see different ways to stop safely. You also learn how to stride and how to turn.

The International In-line Skating Association (IISA) trains instructors. So far, more than 2,000 in-line skating teachers passed the IISA course in the U.S. Check for classes at skate shops, sports centers, or community centers. Local skate clubs may hold clinics or other practice sessions, too.

*Grabbing your partner for support is not always the smart thing to do.*

*Press on your heel and drag the brake pad to stop.*

## START STOPPING FIRST

Before you start on pavement, know how to stop. Falling doesn't count. The most common stopping system uses a heel brake on one skate. Know which skate has the brake pad. It looks like a black rubber square at the rear of your skate.

You drag the brake on the pavement to build **friction**. Friction slows you down. It also wears the brake pad. A small line on the brake shows you when to replace the pad. A pad costs less than $6.

To stop with a heel brake, coast with your skates about shoulder-width apart. Bend your knees. Hold your arms out in front, so you can see your hands. Slowly and firmly press your heel down on your brake skate. Your toe lifts up. This foot moves forward a bit.

Later on, add style by coasting with your non-brake knee tucked into the back of the braking knee. Shift your weight off the non-brake skate and balance on only the front foot.

## LETTER-PERFECT T-STOPS

Instead of brake pads, advanced skaters drag their wheels. Try it when you're ready. Let one foot drag sideways to your front skate in an upside-down T position. Bend your knees with your weight on the front skate. You'll feel shaky and you might not hold the position too long. Try switching which foot you put forward. You might feel more comfortable with one or the other. Mostly, keep practicing!

RAD TIP

**Breaking In Brakes**
You gain more stopping power from a half-worn brake than a new brake. Skaters sometimes saw off the tips of new brakes to skip the breaking-in stage.

# SWIM IN AIR

In-line skating borrows moves, tricks, gear, and even words from hockey, figure skating, roller skating, skiing, and skateboarding. Some people even say it's like swimming in air.

Just like good swimmers, in-line skaters stroke and glide. Face your shoulders forward. Push or stroke to the side with your heel, like you're spreading peanut butter. Flick your heel at the end of the stroke. Imagine the peanut butter is stuck to it and you want to shake it off. Keep the side-to-side movement under your waist.

Better skaters glide on only one skate. It just takes practice. Try to glide on one skate for 3 to 5 seconds, increasing to 30 seconds. Switch feet when you push off. Bend your knees and relax.

Curl your fingers lightly around the wrist guards. Your arms stay close to your body. Pretend you're hauling in a long rope—one hand pulls back, then the next—always reaching forward and swinging back from waist-high. Side-to-side swinging throws you off balance. Swing side to side only when starting out or climbing hills.

# WHERE TO WHEEL

The peaceful and religious Amish allow in-line skating, yet many cities don't. Go figure. Although most in-line skaters use common sense and good manners, a few rude and reckless skaters gave the sport a bad rap. Don't be one of them.

chapter
# THREE

Experts say most 7- or 8-year-olds can handle in-line skating. Grommets, or young skaters, have muscles strong enough for good balance and control. Just as important, they're old enough to know about safety gear, traffic, and road and weather conditions.

## DRIVE CAREFULLY

No matter what age you are, you must obey traffic laws when you travel on wheels—skate wheels included. Stop at stop signs. Signal your turns. Ride on the right. Pass on the left. Let walkers and joggers, and any other **pedestrians**, go first. Watch cars, children, and dogs that might pop out in front of you. Be ready to stop any time.

## START HERE

A flat, smooth, and clean surface works best for new skaters. Indoor skating rinks work great. Some cities let skaters roll through their sports stadium halls.

Outside, look for empty parking lots, tennis courts, or other open areas. Signs **forbidding** skating mean what they say. Most cities give tickets and fines for breaking the law.

If you get lucky and find black ice (a freshly paved street), check it out first. Can you stay clear of cars? Will walkers or joggers cross your path? Can you handle the hills? Even a small slope can build your speed. A big hill can easily launch a skater up to 35 mph (56 kph). Radar guns have clocked skaters flying downhill at more than 75 mph (120 kph)! One pebble or a bit of sand can quickly end the ride. Pay attention!

Use your brake pad to control your speed. Ride it all the way with just slight pressure. Or press on your brake pad every five or ten yards (4.6 or 9.2 m) to slow your pace.

**Basic Rules Of The Road**
1. Stay on the right side of a lane.
2. Say "passing on the left" to anyone you're going to pass—before you pass them.
3. Give pedestrians the right of way. Always!

## DODGE THE DOGS

Dodge the dogs if you can. Sprinting away works well when you can't. Keep your arms and hands close to your body. Squirting water in a dog's face usually makes him stop. Unlike mace, water won't hurt the pooch. Most dogs don't bite and they probably won't follow you past their home turf. You can also report the pests to the police.

Sometimes police wear in-line skates. They patrol city pathways to watch for skaters in trouble. In some cities, volunteers from the National Skate Patrol lend a hand. Look for their red shirts on the main skating routes. They'll even give you skating pointers on the spot.

## MAINTENANCE MATTERS

Check buckles, wheels, brakes, and bearings before and after you skate. Wheels wear down, usually on the inside of the foot. **Rotating** the wheels helps them wear evenly. Terrain, temperature, your weight, and skating style all affect how often you need to rotate. Some people rotate their wheels monthly. Others do it every day.

RAD TIP

**Tune-up**
Bring your skates to a professional for a tune-up every 6 months or so. Most skate shops service what they sell, or they know who will.

**Here's How To Rotate Your Wheels:**

**1.** Using a pen, number your wheels 1 to 4 from toe to heel. Make sure you mark on the same side of the wheels. If you have dark wheels and pen marks won't show, use numbered pieces of tape.

**2.** Remove the wheels and lay them in order from toe to heel.

**3.** Swap the position of wheel 1 with wheel 3, and of wheel 2 with wheel 4 (wheel 1 goes where wheel 3 used to be, wheel 2 goes where wheel 4 used to be.)

**4.** Put the wheels back on the skates in this new order.

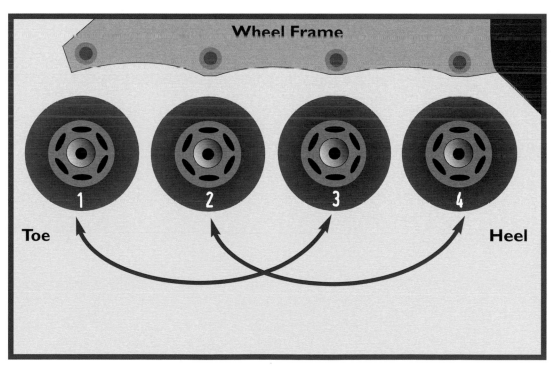

*Skates last longer and perform better when you take care of them.*
*Rotate your wheels often.*

Many things that bikes can ride over will trip skaters up in a hurry. These dangers in the road can also damage your skate wheels and bearings. Never stop scanning the pavement ahead of you for:

- Holes, cracks, sewer covers, and bumps in the pavement
- Puddles, mud, oil, and wet pavement
- Branches, grass, and other debris
- Sand, stones, or loose pavement

A few more safety tips—don't push a baby stroller or run your dog on a leash when you're on your skates. Leave your headphones at home. Hearing a car or train horn could save your life.

# SICK TRICKS

Aggressive skating began almost as soon as better skates appeared in the 1980s. The tricks came directly from skateboarding at first. Both skateboarders and in-line skaters do tricks with "grabs," holding the gear with one hand to give their tricks "style." They both try to throw "sick" tricks, or awesome moves, in the air.

Skateboarders and in-line skaters often clashed at the skate parks in the early years. Boarders thought the skaters barged into the half-pipes, snaking weak tricks instead of taking turns. Now some skateboarders still won't welcome you with hugs, but they'll put up with you.

chapter

FOUR

## STUNT RIDING

In-line skaters started with skateboard tricks, but they soon created hundreds of moves just for skates. You can't even count the different grinds you can do. The names for tricks change across the country, too. You might do a soul grind in California, but the same move is a smith in New York.

Some aggro-skaters focus on **vert** tricks. Vert skaters stay in the skate park, dropping into the half-pipe, a U-shaped ramp built for tricks. "Vert" comes from the vertical, or upright, sides of the ramp. (If the sides were angled instead of upright, skaters would launch right out of the park.) Most vert skaters go for big air. They do grabs and spins high above the **coping**, or edge, of the half-pipe.

## BACK-UP BASICS

Dial in your basic skills before you try tricks. Then start with skating backwards, or fakies. Find flat and open pavement. Roll backwards slowly. Imagine tracing the number 8. Your skates pull in and push out, pull in and push out—over and over again. Try pushing one leg out and rolling on the other. Change feet. Then push left, roll right; push right, roll left. Practice, practice, practice.

RAD TIP

### Stupid Tricks Are Stupid Tricks

Like some skateboarders, some in-line skaters do dumb things. The biggest bone-head move is "truck-surfing" or "skitching," where a skater hangs onto a moving vehicle. Skaters can't match vehicle speed, cornering, or braking power. They crash into the vehicle, get tossed into traffic, or face-plant on the asphalt. Some die.

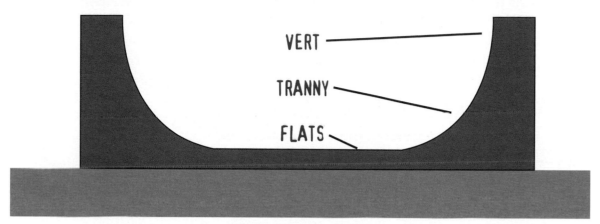

## THE HALF-PIPE

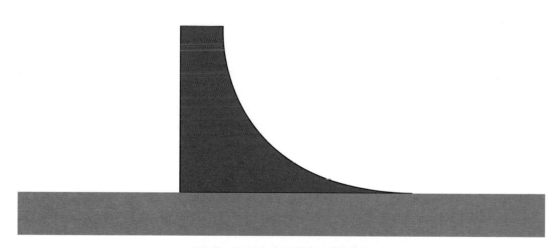

## THE QUARTER-PIPE

*Half-pipes, usually built of wood, range from 3 feet (.92 m) to over 12 feet (2.76 m). Most ramps are a U-shaped half-pipe. A flat base meets the transition walls on each side, forming the curve before the walls go vertical. Ramps can also come in quarter-pipe or launch styles.*

*Work up to dropping in. Know how to pump in the pipe first.*

## PARK SESSIONS

Serious aggro-skaters do daily sessions, or skating time, at the skate park. Half-pipe work takes more practice than you think.

Dropping in, or rolling from the deck into the pipe, causes a lot of face-plants for the beginners. Start from the bottom instead. Roll up to the top and come back down. Then add some pumping. Bend your knees and push out your feet when you come up to the transition. Turn around at the top, then pump again. Swing your arms to build **momentum**. The more you pump, the more air you get.

Once you can roll high enough to pull yourself onto the deck, you can start dropping in. Some skaters sit down on their skates the first time. To drop in standing up, roll your first two wheels over the edge and bend down low. Tip into the pipe, stand up, and ride.

# A FLAIR FOR AIR

Spend a few days at the skate park, and you quickly learn which tricks to try now and which to save for later. Other skaters will point out how to nail some of them. You can also check the web. A few sites explain the details, too. You might see these tricks at your skate park or on the demo (demonstration) tours.

## *INTERMEDIATE*

1. **Cab or Fakie 360** -
The Cab name comes from skateboarder Steve Caballero. He invented the trick and in-line skaters borrowed it. You ride backward up the half-pipe or jump, spin a full circle, and land rolling backwards. A Half-Cab, also from skateboarding, means riding up backward and rotating so that you land facing forward.

## *INTERMEDIATE*

2. **Express Air** -
This trick sounds easier than it is. When you feel yourself launch, grab the inside of the skate with the same hand (right skate, right hand). Add style by kicking the other leg out straight, or stiff. Spot your landing and nail it.

*Kicking your leg out adds style to a trick.*

## 3. Brainless

The name speaks for itself. This trick is a back flip with a 540 (a spin and a half).

(All spins, from a 180 to a 1080, are based on 360 degrees in one full spin. Do the math to figure out how many spins in a trick. What's a 720 (say: seven-twenty)? Two full spins. Get it?

## 4. Hip-Hop

This looks way cool. You flip upside down flying up the ramp and do a handstand, or an invert, on the coping. Some call it a hand plant, too. Touch the coping twice with your hand before you land on your feet and roll it out.

**RAD TIP**

**Talk About Tricky!**
In-line skating has its own language. What's the difference between crossed and crossed-up? Crossed means a grab with one hand reaching to the opposite foot. Crossed-up means the feet cross, not the hands. Look on the web for the latest words and terms.

*Professional ramps use special materials for extra safety and a smooth surface.*

## RAMP UP YOUR YARD

Skateboarders started building ramps at home in the 1970s. They know what they're doing. You'll find proven ideas and plans for ramps in skateboarding magazines and Web sites. These tips apply no matter where you find your plan:

1. Ask permission first. Taking a ramp apart is no fun.
2. Borrow the tools. Bring them back when you're done.
3. Start small. You can add on later. Attach handles or wheels and make them movable.
4. Scrap wood works if you can't afford to buy new.
5. If you don't have a printed plan, sketch your idea on paper first. Include enough bracing. Falling through the deck adds humor for gawkers but no style points.

Wear your armor and have a blast.

## SKATERS WITHOUT A PARK

Street skaters are like vert skaters without a park. They cruise urban areas. They don't do verts, but they still do tricks. They rip grinds on rails and ledges. They bump or ride down stairs. They even pull big air for spins off of any launch.

The biggest street trick of all is finding a place to do it legally. Don't think the skateboarders always know where to go. Police give tickets to skateboarders and in-line skaters alike.

## STREET SESSIONS

Street skaters focus on grinds. The basic grind starts by rolling next to a curb. You jump up and turn 90 degrees, or a quarter-turn, and land with your wheels crossing the curb like a T. Then you slide along sideways. Which foot leads, which side of the foot grinds, which direction you jump from or land on—all of these give you a different grind trick.

Wax the curb or bar to avoid sticking. **Paraffin** wax in your grocer's canning section works just fine. So does melted candle wax and even crayons. Lay on a thick coat. Wax on handrails make it too slippery to land a jump, and it angers local police. Wear your pads. Shred in peace.

*Street skaters grind handrails, curbs, and other city structures.*

# STREET SKATING TRICKS

### 1. Frontside

This is a good starter grind. Roll beside a bar or curb on your right. When you turn 90 degrees to hop on it, turn clockwise, or to your right. Then slide. Most often the Frontside becomes part of more difficult tricks.

### 2. Royale

Also called a Shifty in some places, this grind works the inside edge of one skate and the outside edge of the trailing skate. Keep your knees bent. Look forward but keep your upper body sideways to the rail.

### 3. Rewind

If you can't spin, you can't rewind. As you finish a grind, you do a spin in the opposite direction from which you were facing. A 270 works well, since it takes 90 degrees to pull your body in line with the rail or curb. Then come around halfway (another 180 degrees) and land it fakie.

# WINNING ISN'T EVERYTHING

Winning isn't everything. It's how you look that counts. Clothing and hair aside, the saying holds a bit of truth for in-line skaters. How does your trick look? Is it smooth? Does it have style? Is it your own? Does it look easy when it's really very hard to do? Are you having fun? That's everything.

chapter
# FIVE

## CHAMPION EVENTS

The TV stations broadcast all kinds of in-line skating contests. The Aggressive Skaters Association (ASA) works with ESPN, MTV, NBC, and other partners to show its annual tour of professional championships.

Skaters compete in different events, such as Park (set up like a skate park), Jam (obstacles), Half-Pipe (vert), or Best Trick (session-style). Judges look for style, variety, and control. They reward skaters who show aggressive moves and smooth lines.

Another big contest event, called **Slalom**, challenges racers to move through a line of cones as quickly as they can. Hitting a cone adds time to the racer's run. The fastest time wins.

The ASA also promotes amateur events and demo tours. With a single international organization supporting them, pro in-line skaters enjoy bigger prize money and more fans than other extreme athletes. Amateurs stand a better chance of moving into the spotlight, too.

*Pro and amateur skaters compete in many kinds of events.*
*Rollerblade sponsored this contest.*

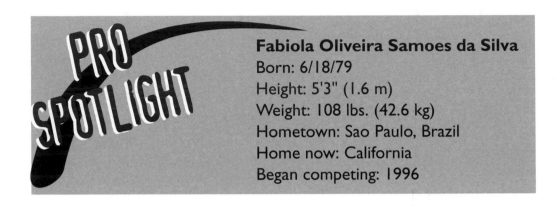

**PRO SPOTLIGHT**

**Fabiola Oliveira Samoes da Silva**
Born: 6/18/79
Height: 5'3" (1.6 m)
Weight: 108 lbs. (42.6 kg)
Hometown: Sao Paulo, Brazil
Home now: California
Began competing: 1996

Called the Queen of the Half-Pipe, beautiful Fabiola ranks as the top female aggressive skater in the world. She holds all the big titles for vert and street events. Skating with the boys in her hometown in Brazil gave her the edge. Instead of competing against females only, Fabiola now enters contests against guys—and comes in among the top five every time!

*Fabulous Fabiola ranks as one of the world's best skaters.*

# ROLLER HOCKEY WINS SKATERS OVER

In-line skating began with hockey players. Returning to its roots, in-line skating now includes some 2 million people of all ages who play roller hockey. They chase a ball or a puck with small wheels on the bottom. The teams try to nail one in the net like the ice skaters do.

Roller hockey rocks with the fast pace of ice hockey. If you can in-line skate, you can play. You don't need much more than a parking lot or a flat paved area for a rink. Hundreds of leagues already exist in the United States. Roller hockey wins over more wheeling skaters all the time.

Sports experts called in-line skating a fad. The sport fought off a rebel image and climbed out from under the shadow of skateboarding. Even with a name that's a chunky mouthful, in-line skating promises to stay a healthy part of the American sports scene.

# FURTHER READING

Your library and the Internet can help you learn more about in-line skating. Check these titles and sites for starters:

Armentrout, David. *Sports Challenge: In-Line Skating*. Rourke Book Co., 1997.

Miller, Cam. *Roller Hockey*. Sterling Publishing Company, 1996.

Miller, Liz. *Get Rolling: The Beginner's Guide to In-Line Skating*. Ragged Mountain Press, 1998.

Zverina, Rogert. ed. *Gear Up! Guide to In-Line Skating*. International In-Line Skating Association.

# WEBSITES TO VISIT

expn.go.com
www.heckler.com
www.inlineskating.about.com
www.aggroskate.com
www.skatefaq.com
www.heckler.com
www.iisa.org
www.aggressive.com
www.rollerblade.com
www.usahockey.com/inline

# GLOSSARY

**aggressive skating** (ah GRES ihv SKAYT ing) — a hard-core style of in-line skating that focuses on performing tricks

**antiseptic** (an tih SEP tik) — a lotion, cream or spray that kills germs

**coping** (KOH ping) — the protective cap on a wall

**forbidding** (for BID ing) — not allowing

**friction** (FRIK shun) — rubbing one surface against another

**helmet** (HEL mit) — also called a brain bucket, this gear protects your skull and brain from injuries

**momentum** (moh MEN tum) — force or speed of movement

**paraffin** (PAYR uh fin) — a wax made from crude oil

**pedestrians** (peh DES tree enz) — people traveling by foot, like walkers or joggers

**retrofit** (reh troh FIT) — replacing or upgrading the original parts with new parts

**rotating** (ROH tayt ing) — change the order or swap positions

**slalom** (SLAH lum) — a race set on a zig zag course marked by orange cones or flags

**stance** (STANS) — the body's position while standing

**terrain** (tah RAYN) — the land or ground

**vert** (VURT) — comes from vertical, meaning upright

**wrist guards** (RIST GAHRDZ) — gear that protects your hands and wrists from snapping backwards or scraping on the asphalt

47

# INDEX

# ABOUT THE AUTHOR

Tracy Nelson Maurer specializes in nonfiction and business writing. Her most recently published children's books include the *A to Z* series, also from Rourke Publishing LLC. An avid in-line skater, she lives with her husband Mike and two children in Superior, Wisconsin.